SONGS OF
ENLIGHTENMENT

ALSO BY ILCHI LEE

Healing Society Trilogy

Healing Society : A Prescription for Global Enlightenment
The 12 Enlightments for Healing Society
Peaceology for Healing Society(spring, 2003)

Brain Respiration : Making Your Brain Creative,
Peaceful, and Productive
Dahnhak : The Way to the Perfect Health
The Way to Light up Your Divinity
Mago's Dream : Communing with the Earth's Soul

SONGS OF
ENLIGHTENMENT

ILCHI LEE

Healing Society

Healing Society

Healing Society, Inc.
7664 W. Lake Mead Blvd. #109
Las Vegas, NV 89128

e-mail:healingsociety@newhuman.org
Web site:www.healingsociety.org

If you are unable to order this book
from your local bookseller,
you may order directly from the publisher.
Call 1-877-324-6425, toll-free.

ISBN 0-9720282-1-8
Library of Congress Control Number: 2002108261

Printed in South Korea

For you

CONTENTS

PART II : HEAVEN & EARTH WITHIN THE HUMAN

PART III : FOR HUMANITY

SONGS OF
ENLIGHTENMENT

PREFACE

My poems

It is said that poets 'compose' poems
But I have never composed a poem.
Poems come to me.
Poets say they 'arrange' poems.
I just write down
Without adornment
Sounds exploding
Colliding within me, shining through me
Life's currents and rhythms
Onto paper.

My poems are not about beauty
About meter or rhyme.
They sketch a self-portrait
About what I do, have done, will do.
A history of Healing Society in Action
For the last twenty years.

My poems reveal enlightenment and belief
Offering comfort and encouragement
To students and fellow travelers.
Messages of the Universe
Written out of love for humanity and the Earth
Delivered through the messenger
That is me.

Enlightenment is the courage
To reveal your life.
Thus I reveal
Without fear
Without shame
The life within me.

Such is the power of my poems.

PART I

EVERY FLOWER THAT BLOSSOMS IS BEAUTIFUL

Divinity

Night filled with inky blackness
Stars whisper in my ear
Twinkling with merriment and delight;
The stars you see above
You see only with eyes.

I had thought so once
That it was I who saw in your eyes
The raindrops pinging on the windows;
Hearing only with ears
The stars and the rain;
Now that I truly open my eyes and ears
I realize that I am myself the stars and the rain.

A bright light sweeps through me
Then I am neither stars nor rain;
Truly realizing myself and all else
Life everlasting and whole
Cannot be formed into words.

Heaven's stars continue to twinkle
Heaven's raindrops continue to fall.

Breath

The breath that I breathe is not mine
It is the breath of the universe
Breath of life
Swirling in the grand breath of Cosmic Mind
Sighing with the soft breathing of Cosmic Energy.
Grass, trees, clouds, people
All the universe dances
To the rhythm of my breathing.

I forsake my weary past
With expulsion of each breath.
With each breathing cycle
I die and am reborn.
I am no longer afraid of death
For death is the bright promise of new life.
I know that were I not to die
I could not be reborn into a new existence.

As I inhale and exhale
I see my existence anew
And recognize the law of the Cosmos.
When I breathe freely
I become one with Heaven
One with the divine.
For I have never been apart
From the heaven, land and sea.

Within this breath
You and I are one,
Not bound by time or space
Nor knowing sorrow and pain,

Living according to the law
Of heaven and earth,
Tasting the sky
Feeling the universe.

Drinking the energy of the universe
Breathing along with the Cosmos
With each breath
I am reborn
Into a brand new existence.
With each breath
The universe begins again
With a brand new wave.

One Love

Oceans open wide
Sails crossing their horizons;
Sea flowers sway in the beating waves
As seagulls cry to the rhythm of the wind
And fishes move in search of prey.

Creation begins from imagination
So do greed and misfortune;
Truth and effort may increase human worth
But they are not enough to make us whole;
Only love can complete us.

Life without love
Is as night without day;
Let love lead you to heaven
To a grand love
That is one love.

Love of the one
In the midst of which
You will become whole;
For in one
You and I are one...
All of life is one.

Travel

In the midst of the starry light,
To the sound of pounding waves,
Guided by Cosmic Energy,
Heading to a place without end,
We walk without reason.

Waves welcome the cool breeze
Without a care in the world,
Along the whispering sand,
Toward a destination without location,
We walk.

Following Cosmic Energy,
Led by Cosmic Mind,
We carry the burden of life,
Buoyed by starlight
Beneath our feet.

Journey of Cosmic Energy,
Path to Cosmic Mind,
Not knowing when it will end,
Nor knowing when it began,
We walk.

As our journey continues
Beyond this life,
We are unable even to recall
Burdens of the past,
Nor anticipate the future.

We don't even know the shape

Or feel the weight
Of this burden that we carry;
The only sure thing
Is that we are companions on the road.

We are married;
Traveling together on this road
Whose end we can't see,
And whose source is unknown.
Companions walking together.

Journey to Oneness,
To teachings of the way;
Until we realize the way of heaven
We will persevere,
We will walk.

ChunJiKiUn(Cosmic Energy),   ChunJiMaEum(Cosmic Mind)

God plays with the Earth
Children play with hoops
Birds play with clouds;

What is the difference
Between God and the children?
Between God and the birds?

Clouds turn to rain and snow
To dampen the ground
Leaves flutter
And fog retreats against the wind;

As flowers turn to fruit
Fruit becomes the tree;
Children become adults
Adults are reborn as children;

In the sky above,
Along the path
Of the wind and the rain,
So go the clouds
So goes my heart.

# I Know You

Do not cringe so
Now get up and run
You can do it
One single failure
Is not your all
Cast your dreams
With all your might.

Do not cower so
The sadness you hold inside
Is no big deal
Water under the bridge.

Open your heart wide
And show me your truth
Your infinite possibilities and dreams
Showing the real you
Whom I see.

Do not shrivel so
For I do not care for it
If you lack a dream
Let me be your dream.

I know you...
That you hold inside
Vast possibilities and dreams
And limitless love.

You can do it
You have warmth in your heart.

I am your soul!
I am your soul!

The Secret of the Golden Flower

Inside your heart
A golden flower blossoms;
Inside of me
And inside of you
Never dying...
This flower of your soul
Most precious gift
Bestowed by God;
Its' golden scent
Offers a lifetime of love
To dwell in your heart forever
Blossoming
Unconditionally
Without judgment
Surrounding you
With absolute purity and love.

This flower is not for others
For you alone
It comes alive
Only in the hands of its own gardener;
Inside of everyone
This flower is waiting
Regardless of riches or fame
It waits for all;
As you leave this earth
Another awaits its' beauty;
Approach and say
I have nurtured this flower,
Loaned to me
I now give it to you,

Golden flower
Hidden deep inside.

I found this flower so filled with love.

Your...

Your face
Forever holding a joyous smile,
Your arms
Majestic as a crane's wings,
Your heart
Fiery as a dragon's breath,
Your legs
Sturdy as a stately oak,
Your neck
Graceful as a fawn's bow.

Your eyes
Pierce the emptiness yonder
To draw a world of visions and dreams
Beautiful.

Your head
Lights the darkness beyond
Wearing a crown of wisdom
Radiant.

Your body
Dances through the clouds above
Streaking across the sky
Limitless.

Your heart
Beats the roar of a lion
Overflowing with an unstoppable will
Calling.

Your hands
Soothing the pain of humanity
Hands of a bodhisattva
Healing.

Your feet
Fleeting as the fastest steed
Never tiring
Always.

With a grand will deep within your heart,
Your eyes fixed upon the vision,
Confidence and peace dawn on your face,
Power infuses your being.

My Mind Is Heaven

Someone once said
That life is a flower
That withers once it blooms.

My mind is heaven
My eyes are the sun and the moon
My awareness streaks across the darkness
Like the morning star.

My two feet planted firmly in reality
My head moving
In search of the ideal.

My mind is heaven
My eyes are the sun and the moon
My awareness shines like the morning star.

This World Is Beautiful

World sparkles beautifully
Sun shines warmly
Stars twinkle brightly
Moon glows lovingly
Upon all
Upon everyone
Upon everything
God's blessings
Upon us.

Come sadness
Come joy
Come grief
Come happiness
Upon all
Upon everyone
Upon everything
God's blessings
Upon us.

Nothing of heaven or earth
Can take this heart
Filled with love
Nothing of heaven or earth
Can divide us
From cosmic energy
Our vision and hopes
Are our sun our moon our stars.

We can do this
We shall do this...

With eyes and lips closed
Despair and darkness
Stole over us
But we can now see and speak.

Now we know
Limitations are possibilities...
Opportunities to perceive ourselves
Beyond our present selves...

Our loved ones
Wait for us at the doorstep
Of the world of harmony
Forever and lasting
Like the sun, moon, and stars
Oneness.

I am with my loved ones
As we all are with our loved ones.

Meeting You...

My soul
On a starry night
Saw your soul bathed in moonlight;
Forgetting our bodies
We danced in waves of silver
Our souls were free;
I within you
And you within me
Your soul and mine
Traveled the rivers of time;
In meeting you
I knew true joy
Recognized true happiness
And realized true freedom;
By becoming one with you
My divinity
Like the stars in the sky
I could finally twinkle.

White Dragon

I am a white dragon
Invisible to the eye;

I live deep in the ocean
And dwell hidden in the clouds;

My home is nothingness
Everywhere and forever;

I listen to music of the cosmos
And sing songs of the soul;

I belong nowhere
Attached to nothing;

Stars sparkle
Winds blow quietly;

I breathe with the children
Wrapping myself around Bell Rock;

I am cosmic energy
I am cosmic mind.

Eternal Love

Sun, moon, stars
Brighten my soul
Soothe my soul;

When the sun fades... then the moon
When the moon disappears... then the stars
Embrace the world with their never-ending light;

Light is filled
With God's love
In darkness and light
God's love is eternal.

Light of Truth

Not knowing, at all
What life means
How shall I live?
Why does the moon rise into the night sky
And sun shine through the day?

Oh, Creator
Ah, Life
Show me the truth
Guide me to truth
Send me a teacher of truth
Truth is my life, my love.

Walk with me
Along this path
Till the everlasting day
Of perfection immutable
Of completion eternal
When I shall love this path.

My path ... a thousand blessings upon my path
You are truth, life, and love
Enfolding me, unseen yet felt
Bright, liberating light
Light of life ...
Light of truth.

Tears of Joy

Exploding in emptiness
Fragments scatter all around,
Pieces of my shell
Shell of prejudice
Shell of preconceptions
Shell of who I thought I was.
Watching, I cry
Tears of joy.

Colliding with the bright light
Of my true self,
My illusions scream loudly,
Themselves illusions
Created by other illusions,
Finally knowing that
Deep within me
Beneath the shell
Lies the sacred beauty
Of my true self.

I am stunned
At the joy of knowing
My energy is cosmic energy
Cosmic Energy is my energy,
My mind, cosmic mind
Cosmic mind, my mind.

Surrounded thus by my true self
Eternal, holy and bright,
My mouth, ears and eyes gone,
Mouth that speaks not,

Ears that hear not,
Eyes that see not,
I feel you within me,
My eternal reality and true self.
I shall realize peace and harmony on Earth!

Dahn Mu (Energy Dance)

Heaven is dancing
Dancing and laughing,
Ocean and land
Are dancing along,
Undulating to the breath of the sky;

My heart is moving
And singing,
My body coiled with strength,
My limbs filled with power
Like a dragon about to fly;

Heaven is singing
With the mountains and sky,
My body moving silently
To the rhythm of nature,
As my heart listens to Heaven's voice;

Skin touching nature's warmth,
I am one with heaven and earth
As I sing
As I dance
As I cry;

My life
Conversing intimately
With all life,
Heaven is me
As I am heaven,
Nature is me
As I am nature;

Let the karma of a thousand lifetimes
Unravel in ones and twos
Through the dance of life
Dahn Mu.

This Is Love

Petals scatter in the breeze
Teasing me;
You could give me everything in the world
Yet I could not live without you.

I go with the clouds
I go with the wind
Yes, that is love. Love.
We are all in this together
Joined in the beauty of love
Yes, that is love. Love.
We are in this together.

Stars wink in the night sky,
Moon lays bare my heart,
Memories of love dazzle,
Raising its curtain of longing.

I go with the clouds
I go with the wind
Yes, that is love. Love.
We are all in this together
Joined in the beauty of love
Yes, that is love. Love.
We are all in this together.

With the wind and clouds
Go I...
Goes my love...
For higher love
Go we all.

World of harmony and peace
I see it just over there
Right there.

White Clouds in the Blue Sky

I want to be the sky
Embracing all that I see
Clouds, moon, sun, mountains and rivers
Holding close all that I feel;

I want to be the clouds
Bestowing rain where parched
Going where the wind takes me
Flowing freely;

I want to be the moon
Listening to the prayers of good people
Cherished as a beautiful memory
In the hearts of lovers
A full moon swinging low
On a shimmering black chariot;

I want to be the wind
Caressing birds, trees and sweating farmers
Whispering, refreshing all
An invisible hand on the shoulder
Comforting;

I want to be the sun
To be the stars
No, not any of these
I want to be life itself
Belonging to no one
Being nothing...
True self;

Clouds roll across the blue sky
Birds chatter noisily in the hills
Waves pound the beaches
Young children play merrily
Across the wide field
And beyond distant hills
The whistle of a train
Drifts in the breeze
Lingering.

The Heavenly Maiden

Snow flakes falling through the blue sky
Become flowers giving joy to all.
Leaves falling in autumn become nectar
For people who are lonely.
The beauty of a maiden's heart
Is more beautiful than a lotus flower.

What karma melts snow fallen to earth
To flow again as water in a stream?
What karma piles snow onto a pine branch
To breathe its' eternal scent?

Your beauty as it blossoms through time...
More magnificent than a lotus flower,
Your fragrance piercing the soul
More awakening than coffee's aroma,
Your love shimmering in the sunlight
Scarlet, as a ripe cherry.

Flower that blooms within one
In one come hither
In one live forever.
Hearts that beat within one
In one come together
Let body and energy join forever.

Solitary Pine Tree

A solitary pine
Is alone but never sad
And always proud
Proud in its essence;

Its scent
Arises from its faith
Emerges from its discipline
Transpires from its' will;

A thousand year old white crane
Attains inestimable beauty
Because it has transcended
Material delights;

An enlightened man
Likes the pine, the crane and the rock.

True Love

Love is beautiful
Powerfully addictive
Paralyzing logic
Banishing fear
Erasing loneliness
Obliterating self-consciousness
Embracing shyness
Imparting courage.

Love is selfish
Seeding hatred and tears
Turning people into knives
Cutting wounds into lovers' hearts
Inflicting pain, grief and despair.

To know the face of true love
Requires time
Your hair frosts over
Your eyes and ears dull.

When you realize
That love is not ego
And cannot be possessed
Your body is cold
Your skin marred with age.

Then your eyes open
To new possibilities of love
Neither hot nor cold
Full of grace and forgiveness.

Loves' essence blossoms
With respect
Its' gentle fragrance sustains the soul
Let us open our eyes
To true love.

PART II

Heven and Earth within The Human

Hills Are Deep, Rivers Run High

Hills are deep
Rivers run high.

A babe's legs are as thick as tree trunks
While the general's arms remain spindly.

A thousand-year-old dragon
Is swallowed whole by a tadpole.

The crescent moon shines brighter than the full moon
From whence does it illuminate the earth?

When someone asks what this all means
Tell him... the infant runs while the mother crawls.

Old authority shall make way for new ideas
Material civilization shall be replaced by a spiritual one.

Finding True Self

Everyone has it
To know what it is.
Take a journey deep within
And open your eyes wide.
Then you will see everything.

Even without knowing why and how,
Everyone has it in one's heart.
Someday, you will see it.
Someday, you will see it.

Everyone has it
Remembering what it is.
As if it had been in a deep sleep,
What I have been is not what I have aspired to be,
Nor what I can be.
But now I can see it well,
I can see it through tears in my eyes.

Now I have the ticket to the stage of my life in my hands.
Though I am only halfway there,
I see there is a great possibility and light at the end.

Now more and more people are beginning to awaken
        as I have,
Yes, it really is a good thing.

Now more and more people are beginning to see what
        I see,
Yes, it really is a good thing.

Journey of Discipline

We have come
To train
Upon the training grounds
Of the world.

Patience, forgiveness and love
Paths to awareness
God's gifts to all
Provided in this environment.

Body, personality, relationships
Environment and time
All tasks given to me
Are given out of love.

A tree does not complain
That the earth is too dry or too rough
That the rains do not come often
With patience, forgiveness and harmony
It does its best ... fulfilling its mission.

The mountain is sacred
It does not differentiate
Nor discriminate
Whatever the tree may be
Whenever the rains may come
Wherever lightening may strike
However the wind may blow
Welcoming all
Embracing all
With patience, forgiveness and love.

Flower of Harmony

Do not dwell in the past
Nor flow into the future,
Feel the cosmic energy here and now
Create a paradise of heaven and peace
Within the cosmic mind...

Drowning in a sea of attachments
Future, past and present are mere nightmares,
Plans and dreams
Cannot impart the Tao to self and others
They are neither Zen nor Truth.

With an empty mind
Study what you have been given,
Without delay
Study of Principles
Study of Practice
Study of Living
Then you have arrived at Jung-Ji.

Flowers of harmony blossom naturally
In a field of appreciation,
Be a gardener and tend to the flowers
To become a true star of life,
For then you will be a lighthouse
Guiding others home,
You will be a panacea
Healing others wherever you go,
You will have become
A new human.

Jung-ji signifies the 3rd step in the 9 steps to enlightenment in which the soul has come alive to allow you to experience the pure consciousness and true self within you, readying you to begin the main stage of practice.

Drink in the Heaven, Eat of the Earth

Human roots lie in heaven and earth
The parents of humanity.
Through your nose drink in the heavens
With your mouth partake of the earth
And let heaven and earth light up your mind and
      spirit.

To enlighten your mind and inspire your spirit,
To become divine
You must complete the journey.
For those who do not complete the journey
Though on a diet of heaven and earth
Are but ghosts of themselves.

Human worth lies in completion
Material completes the form
Ethics nurture the mind.
We exist to become complete
Complete unto God.

Heaven and earth lie within the human,
We are the masters of all.
Ah, young fools,
Don't you know...
You have an inheritance
Of heaven and earth.

Light of the True Self (1)

I know no day or night;
Night descends when I close my eyes
Day returns when I open them;
I was born to communicate enlightenment to all.

All my ego's prejudices and presumptions
Nothing but scattered dark clouds
Covering the sun of which I am.
Watching the Creator
In love... great and magnificent
Sun has no day or night
For only light exists;
It only depends on where you stand.

With the light of my true self guiding me
I see clearly
Who has created the universe,
Going freely beyond time and space
As I stand with the Creator.

I see countless souls there
Many sages and saints;
Divinity that I am
Born on Earth
To realize a world of harmony and peace;
I am cosmic energy and cosmic mind;
I have arrived and found

My true self.

Light of the True Self (2)

Here but there
Seeing but invisible
Sleeping but awake
Touching but empty;
Just as a seagull skims the water
Does spring miss the flowers
Or flowers long for spring?

Enlightenment flashes
A momentary apparition
Gone in the next moment;
Ah, but the moment is forever
Or perhaps forever exists within the moment;
Happiness and peace exist only in the moment
Felt now... then gone;
As we pursue security, peace, happiness and freedom
Our senses blink like the stars,
Awareness jumping perilously
Moment to moment.

A moment is forever
And forever is but a moment;
A line is a collection of dots
And life, an amalgam of cells;
Energy is just another language that connects all life;
Birth and death are natural phenomena of energy;
Attachments create isolation
From the living current of energy.

Attachments are obstacles to enlightenment
Stealing freedom and peace;

And it is only through enlightenment
That true self will shine forth.

Message of Cosmic Energy

ChunJiKiUn brings
Health of body and peace of mind;

ChunJiKiUn erases
Loneliness and grief;

ChunJiKiUn gives
Confidence and pride;

ChunJiKiUn fills your heart
With love overflowing;

ChunJiKiUn gives you the strength
To forgive those who cause you pain;

ChunJiKiUn knows no fear
Feels no terror;

ChunJiKiUn allows no ego or conceit
Makes you industrious, responsible and honest;

ChunJiKiUn purifies the spirit
And nurtures the soul, leading to eternal life;

Sacred energy of ChunBuSung
The sacred energy of the universe is ChunJiKiUn.

ChunJiKiUn is the Korean term for Cosmic Energy.
ChunBuSung is the home star of the soul, signifying the center of
the multi-dimensional universe.

Golden Bird

Once creatures of the ground,
We were sightless,
Wandering in the dark
Filled with desperation and despair.

Falsely led by greed and shallow hunger,
Burrowing like a bug into the soil,
We lived in a dim world of gloom
Filled with anxiety and fear.

Little peace and happiness existed;
We could not be satisfied,
Unable to share the glory of the sun
Or feel the joy of freedom.

Yearning for truth of light and freedom,
We longed to spread our wings and fly forth
And greet the grand sight of the open air
With strength and joy in our hearts.

This is why we seek to be
As a bird
With golden wings.
Fly forth and share the glory of the sun.

Heavenly Transformation

A caterpillar becomes a moth
And a silkworm is transformed into a butterfly
Who knew?
That a moth was waiting in a caterpillar
And a butterfly lay hidden in a silkworm.

Who knew?
Divinity lay within humanity
Evolving into God
On the road called
The Tao of Heavenly Transformation (ChunHwa)
Now forgotten ages ago.

Brothers feuding
Children disobeying parents
Students betraying teachers
Nations invading and killing
Religions fighting
Ideologies conflicting
An age of sin.

Purity and love have gone
Diminished by collusion and treachery;
People are enslaved
By selfishness and conceit.

Heaven, earth and stars alike
Are ravaged by disease;
Darkness is the lot
Of those who have lost divinity within;
Oppressive silence is the norm

Of humans possessed by greed;
Humans no longer know heaven and earth,
Disregarding parents, brothers and teachers.

With the path of Heavenly Transformation
        (ChunHwa) lost,
Happiness and true peace
Are wandering in darkness;
Tao of Heavenly Transformation (ChunHwa)
Last hope for salvation
For humanity
For heaven
For earth.

The Tao of Heavenly Transformation (ChunHwa)
Essence of Dahnhak.

Egotism

If you desire health
Put your ego aside;
If you desire happiness
Throw your ego away;
If you desire peace of mind
Cast your ego to the wind;
If you desire true love
Leave your ego behind.

Where ego resides
Worry and anxiety follow;
If you want to be rich
Get rid of your ego;
If you want enlightenment
Rise above your ego.

Where ego prospers
Friends and loved ones will not visit;
If you want to live honestly
Let go of your ego;
If you want to live conscientiously
Banish your ego;
Without ego...
The light of heaven and earth will shine.

Conceit

Conceit
So insignificant
Can destroy a relationship
Drive away a friend.

Conceit
So trivial
Attracts worry and anxiety
As a hyena to death.

Am I pretty?
Am I smart?
Am I rich or on my way?
Am I cool or am I hot?

Strength of character
Seeps away in the cesspool of conceit
Force of will
Moans in pain, obscured.

For love
Let go of ego
For peace of mind
Let go.

Hurry! Hurry!

Insecurity reigns
Joy runs away
Obsession
Mania
Envy and jealousy
Passions erupt
Blood spills.

Keep up with the Joneses
Earn more than your brother
Look prettier than your sister
A morass of competition
A living hell
Filled with the stench of darkness.

Let us get away from such hell
Hurry! Hurry!

Curse of Judgment

Having eaten the fruit
Of the tree of knowledge
Of good and evil
They doubted and forsook
Their promise with God
Learning to differentiate
To judge
To separate.

Wielding the sword of judgment
Blade glinting with sin
Cain killed Abel
In envy and anger
Ego begat jealousy
Jealousy begat betrayal
Betrayal begat murder.

From whence came Ego
Judgment and separation?
From foolishness
Foolish selfishness.

Let us renew our souls with acceptance
Let us rejuvenate our spirit
Such is the way of the Tao
Of Heavenly Transformation (ChunHwa).

Let us all
Rediscover the path
Of Heavenly Transformation
To Enlightenment.

A Poet

To be a poet
You must have loved;
To have said good-bye
To have been betrayed;

Write a poem in despair
And the poem will die;
Write a poem above despair
And the poem will breathe.

Tao is...

Tao is not needed
When you live alone;

Tao is the essence of
Fair transaction, healthy order;

Tao is the light
Showing the way to the New Human;

Tao is the shortcut
To a happy family;

Tao is the bridge
To a healthy society;

Tao is the roof
Over a harmonious civilization;

Tao is the crutch
We lean on towards completion;

Tao is the elixir
For eternal life.

Your Soul

I glimpsed your soul!
In darkness, in wintry cold
A runaway child shivering
Lonely and afraid;

Do you know
Why you feel fear
Or envy
Anger or hatred?

Forgetting your soul
Knowing only your body
Your soul suffers
From abandonment;

Only you can save your soul
Give it home and warmth
Your soul is love, peace and plenty
Creation itself;

Your soul grows
As do you
I love your soul
I await your growth.

Who am I? (1)

I have known
Hypocrisy and falsehood
Sin and depravity
Beauty and honesty
Freedom and deliverance.

I don't wrap myself
In good or evil
Nor disguise myself with authority,
Nobility or even love;
I am who I am.

Loving and angry
I sometimes fast;
I don't care about the clothes I wear
Sneakers and shoes
Korean clothes or western suits
Whatever.

I seek what I need
But do not hunger for riches;
I never have lied or swindled for money;
I do my work
And accept my reward
Head held high.

Recognition comes as
A by-product of my work;
I don't demand authority;
Like clothing and shoes
Whatever.

Sometimes people bow to me thrice
At times I accept
Other times I refuse
Usually a handshake is enough.

Gentlemen of Old
For prestige and honor
Wore furs in summer
Walked when it rained;
Masters of lore
For spiritual purity
Abandoned families and lived harshly
Proud to suffer in vain.

Scorn upon any attempt to pigeonhole
What a master should be
Upon criticism of those who seek a path
Where they fear to tread.

Made by those who choose a master
Acknowledging and anointing another
Self-congratulating in hypocrisy
Fulfilled by vicarious mastership.

Cosmos forever changes
Saints and sages
Watch the master see
The eternal law of life.

What is natural is Tao
Tao knows no falsehood
Does not recognize good or evil
Tao is ever changing and harmonious

Aware of its own eternity.

I cannot be defined
I accept my mission
With sincerity
I declare myself as myself.

Not one bit better
Not one iota worse
Just me as I am
No wrapping paper
By nature, neither pope nor president.

I have walked a difficult road
At times lost and wandering
To find myself
True self that I will keep.

Upon a bright star I have seen my soul;
I will brighten the universe
For I know
That I am light and truth
Cosmic energy and cosmic mind.

To be an enlightened master
Cannot be the privilege
Of a few exceptional souls
Extraordinary in ordinariness;
A Master is honest and filled with common sense.

An ordinary person
Ordinary and complete
Bearing witness to natural perfection
Reveling in ordinary completion.

Ask Your Brain

If you want to know
Why you were born
Ask your brain.
Any difficulties you face
Any problems you need to solve
Kindly and humbly
Ask your brain.

Your brain is the father of computers.
In your brain
Live hope and belief
Enlightenment and peace too.
Past and future
Heaven and hell
Are all in your brain.

Adoration of the Soul

I am a beautiful and innocent soul
I came from a sacred star;

The star of my birth
Bears the name ChunBuSung;

Many souls, beautiful and pure, inhabit this star
In harmony and with delight;

I came to the Earth
To love her and all of life;

When I am finished on Earth
I shall return to ChunBuSung;

I have met many friends on Earth
That I knew back home;

With them I seek
To make Earth healthy;

Everything is in the brain
Everything is in the brain;

ChunBuSung shines with a golden light
My brain shines with a golden light.

To My Disciple, Byukun

Tireless in your efforts
Byukun, disciple that I love
Along countless difficult roads
Through silent hours of solitude
You have been by my side;

Without need or want
Content to remain in my shadow
Keeping the faith in Truth
Communicating enlightenment
Uncomplaining and steady
This I know;

The laborious beating of your heart
Your sorrows and your loneliness
I have heard and felt them all
Perhaps not through words
But with our hearts
I know that we are one;

For more than ten years
You have been my loyal disciple!
I now send to you
A lotus flower of my heart;

When the flower fills your heart
With its' undying scent
The day of harmony will dawn
Beckoning to the chariot of Yuln'yo
To come bear you away
For a well deserved rest.

Yuln'yo is the Korean term designating the all-encompassing harmony and rhythm of cosmos.

Poem of Life

Sensing mystery
From whence did life come?
The flame of life
Bright and beautiful
Too large for the human vessel.

Sea of life
Hills and valleys of life
Sky of life
The flickering glow of the firefly
Sings of mystery
Indefinable.

What is reality?
Do you know?
The fireflies' sparkling flash
Moment to moment
Into eternity
Exists life, life!

To my disciples, whom I love
I give you the gift of the poem of life.

If You Empty Your Head

Buzzing insects live in a pond
In your head
Driving you deeper
Into a confusing morass.

Voice of your soul
Obscured by the roar
Silenced
Makes me sad.

Eyes of your soul
Blinded
By flickering wings
Cannot peer into heaven.

Ears of your soul
Jammed by the buzzing wings
Cannot hear the music of heaven
Makes my heart ache.

Insects of greed
Bugs of gluttony
Obscuring our path
Makes me angry.

Sun's love, star's solitude, moon's silence, earth's
     suffering
All life, all humanity
I embrace
Forever.

Clear your head
Of greed and prejudice
Accumulated over thousands of years
Its hallowed halls muddied.

Empty your head
Become one with heaven, cosmos and me
Cosmic energy and cosmic mind
Eternal life.

Prayer

God in heaven
We are grateful
God in the hills and rivers
We are grateful
God in our hearts
Thy will be done.

We are grateful
For the souls given us
So we may know you
Without eyes or ears.

God in the heart of One World
Thy will be done
God in the hearts of all Earth-Humans
Let us honor you throughout eternity
God, our teacher and servant
Teach us completion
That we may realize peace.

We are grateful
To reside in thy light
Heavenly Father
That thy will be done
Here on earth as it is in heaven
We offer this prayer
In the name of harmony
Of One World.

PART III

FOR HUMANITY

Song of the Earth

Chaos reigned with terrible beauty
Dark and cold
Followed by fire of cosmic magnitude
Searing and bright
Conquered by the will of time
Creating order through Yuln'yo
Bringing order to confusion
Creating the beauty of starry lights
Stunning embroidery of universal fabric.

Life flashed through the peace
Flourishing
Oceans sequestered the mystery of life
Soon revealed in all its glory
Formed into trees and flowers
Insects and animals
Creating harmony
Of cacophonous cries
Of life on Earth.

A deep emerald of the universe
Wearing a mantle fit for a God
More beautiful for its flaws
Of the seas of lapis lazuli
Precious to Father Sun
Dearest to Mother Moon
On a manger of cosmic love
Earth prospered.

With natural rhythm
Rising and falling

Earth prospered through all
Facing the challenges of time
Now a new challenge must be faced
For seven winters have passed
To herald a new era.

Era of insects gone
Era of the lizards vanished
Buried under the will of heaven
Era of humanity has begun
Wearing skins of animals
We passed through the Stone Age
Marched on to the Bronze Age
And fell into darkness of the Middle Ages.

Following our mothers
Respecting our fathers
Worshipping our gods
We feared nature's power
Floods and storms shook our lives
Mercy, we did not expect from the cold
Lightening, thunder, fire and rain
Ignorant of nature
Blaming evil, we appeased gods
Numerous and petty,
Indifferent to human suffering.

No reason seemed to exist
For precious blood spilt for untold sacrifices
Why did my son have to die?
Why did my daughter drown?
No one knew
Except for the gods
To whom we prayed for deliverance from fear,

Ignorance and suffering
Thus we prayed
And our prayers were answered
With the arrival of messengers.

Awakened souls communed with gods
Recording the sacred messages
Out of which religions arose
From families to tribes
Tribes to nations
Superstition to religion
All devised for security
And peace of humanity.

Families feuded
Tribes spilled blood
Striking sparks of conflict
Still consuming the world today
Peace against peace
Security against security
Competition run amuck.

Fists became swords
As spears became guns
Inventions both fantastic and inane
Amazing and amusing
Proliferated
Nurtured by human anxiety
For safety and future
Feeding on desire
For security and peace.

Shocked speechless by the First World War,
The Second numbed us senseless

Must there be a Third?
As blood has been shed
As our homes have been destroyed
Our desire for peace has never been greater.

Who is our greatest enemy?
First nature
With her fury and anger
Then came the beasts
Their roar sent us trembling
Then nations and religions
Disasters of our own making
Now comes the misery of pollution
The devastation of nature
And the earth, our life source
Faces a life-threatening crisis.

Seven great crises before
Were overcome through deep rest
Healing, and purifying
Alas, the eighth crisis today
Shall signal the final end of Earth
Destroying the order of the solar system
Bringing catastrophe to the cosmos
The future is our choice
As God willed it long ago.

Enlightened ones now appear
One by One
Knowing the Earth
Knowing the Mother
Voices of the cosmos embodying hope
Of the Earth, the Sun and Universe
Bless them God

Grant them courage
The knowing courage of enlightenment.

Healing Society has begun
To save the Earth
Closing the curtain
On the age of materialism
Ushering in the era
Of a spiritual civilization.

Pilgrimage

God of all humanity
Embodiment of peace and love
We recognize thy will, thy love
In the messengers of peace
Thou art love;

Aid us in our desire
Bless us in our effort
To create
All-encompassing love;

Let the power of thy love
Awaken in the hearts of all people
The recognition of Oneness
Of humanity
Of Truth;

Grant us thy blessing
To unite
Religions and peoples of the earth
To realize thy love
Together.

Message of Enlightenment

From cosmos came my soul
Earth houses my body;
In a cosmic bungee jump at an appointed time
I landed in the bosom of Mother Earth;
From the womb of my mother
In the warmth of her love
With a loud cry of nine months
I announced my safe arrival on Earth.

Receiving a name for my body
In ignorance
I became the citizen of a nation
Instead of the Earth.

Years have passed
Knowing the Earth
Her beauty, her size
Her true meaning
Friends and teachers coming and going
Leaving me lost and wondering
Until I discovered my own reality.

The meaning of my existence
Of family and nation
Religion and the soul
And Life.

I give thanks
To those who have guided me
To the Creator who sent me
To this important juncture

To awaken
To the task of my life.

Earth's pristine beauty
Is polluted and diseased
Who but humanity
Can heal and purify her?
I am compelled to be a warrior
For a culture of harmony.

I share with all this enlightenment
Already in their hearts;
Knowing that to save the Earth
To keep the Earth
I must fully and unreservedly
Serve.

To create a harmonious civilization
A path of higher consciousness
Working in concert with Humanity
To heal the diseased Earth
To save our home
This road I have chosen.

I swear upon my enlightenment
Of my purpose in life
To give my all and beyond
To found the SUN
And return to my home in the cosmos
As the light, as the ray
Shining with brightness never forgotten
In my home of ChunBuSung.

I am an Earth-Human

I am a New Human
I am a HongIkInGan.

SUN stands for Spiritual United Nations.

This poem came to me while preparing the Prayer of Peace to be read aloud during the opening ceremony of the Millennium World Peace Summit of Religious and Spiritual Leaders. The image of bungee jumping led me to delve into the essence of the source of life, death, and enlightenment.

Let Me Be...

Let me be light eternal
Invisible to the eye
But evident to the heart
Not too far
Nor too near
Remembered not to the eye
But evoked in the heart.

Allow me to be a leader
But not a despot;
For humanity shall no longer
Suffer the indignities of
Tyrants' boots
Of faith nor might.

For a true Teacher
Shall not allow disciples to remain disciples
But push them to new heights
From which they may teach
The Teacher.

Permit me to become the pointing finger
Guiding the lost and wandering
Not blocking the light
That illuminates the path;
Let me radiate a soft glow
For those in darkness
Allow me to be not just a mere cane
To assist the blind forever
But allow me to become a healer
To banish blindness forever;

Allow me the wisdom of a wise doctor
To focus on the patient
And not obsess over the disease.

Let me be light that shines in the darkness;
Let me not cast a shadow on the sun
Knowing that divine joy
Lies in transforming the human
Into God.

Heavenly Medicine

I have in my hands
Medicine to save the world
Yet no jar to hold it
A fire burning.

If you have the courage
To bring me the whiskers of the lord of hell
Come here, come all
I shall make you my sons and daughters.

If you have the audacity
To steal the gates
Of the palace of the lord of heaven
Come, I shall make you my sons and daughters.

Heaven is collapsing
I have the pillars
Yet no one to put them in place
What a tragedy.

Dogs exist aplenty
Loyal to masters
Unafraid of enemies;
People exist aplenty
Taking the lead for a prize
Yet invisible when difficulties arise.

Transcending riches and fame
Respecting all
Maintaining peace of mind
Where are you my friend?

I wrote this poem when feeling at a loss for fellow partners in my work to communicate enlightenment to all.

Enlightenment

In dreamless slumber
Deep in a silent sea
Our divinity lies sleeping
In whom shall it awaken to save the world?

Darkness is not dark
Light is not light
Cosmic radiance lights the world
Sun's warmth revives life.

Birds chirp endlessly in the hills
Flowers sing of the joy of life
Wherever I go
Butterflies dance to the rhythm of life
Making it ever more beautiful.

Who can say
Who corrupted and darkened this beautiful world?
Who can say
Who polluted this world with poison and death?
Who can say
Who allowed this to happen?
Who can say
Who caused this desolation?
Who can say
How far the sickness reaches?
Who has done this?

No one can claim the right
To destroy the profoundly beautiful
Yet people engage in foolish destruction

Wearing masks of idiocy.

Unless divinity rises above
The foam of the dreamless sea
None can save this world
Not God, nor Buddha,
Nor art, nor science, nor philosophy...

The day of resurrection
Will only be
When divinity rises above
The pounding waves
Of the dreamless sea.

Who Am I? (2)

Who am I?
I did not know
Who am I?
I was fooled
Who am I?
Thinking I was my name
Believing my personality to be me
I was wrapped up in who I thought I was.

To know who I really am
Peace, love infinite
All invisible and intangible
Wearing a blindfold I was
Made of ego and greed.

Who gave me name and personality
Feeding and nurturing them,
Giving them comfort in foolishness?
My parents and teachers
My nation and religion
My people
Colluding in foolishness.
Ah, my heartache
My grief
A voice of despair deep within
But unbeknownst to me
A shiny sliver of light
Watched over me.

Voice of soul, life of soul
Infinite life, great and eternal

Existing before personality and character
Light, inestimable and endless
Shocking in brightness;
The earth has taught me
The universe given me confidence;
Things we learn and things we teach
Of nation, religion, and family
How feeble and lacking
Compared to the magnificence of Earth.

With eyes of the soul open
We can feel the earth's love
We can feel the love of the universe;
To see and feel the light and life of the soul
Through the ears, eyes and mind within
This is enlightenment
This is the greatest gift of the Creator.

Now the light is shining
Life is moving
With voice, message and sound
I can hear the song of Arirang
Word before word
Sound before sound
Expressing the joy of enlightenment.

'Ah' is True Self, light and life of the soul
'Ah' cries the babe, proudly announcing
Its' birth to the world;
Alas, the world is filled with those
Deaf to the sound of life
Deaf to the sound of 'Ah.'

'Ah', is recognized only by 'Ri'

Signifying enlightenment
For only enlightenment will allow us
To witness life;
If you know 'Ah'
You are a New Human;
If you can feel 'Ah'
You are in a world of harmony;
The joy, the joy
How can we not be joyful?

We cry out our joy with 'Rang'
Joyful 'Rang,' happy 'Rang.'
A joyful trinity of Arirang
Deep and precious.

Arirang, Arirang, Arariyo
Let us ascend the hills of Arirang;
Earth is the training ground for our soul
Life is a process of climbing over the hills of Arirang;
To cast away the 'Ah' of the true me
And live for name and personality
How thoughtless, how foolish.

If you leave me and go away
Your feet will hurt before you've gone ten miles;
Ten signifies closure, world of completion;
Ignorant of the truth
Going away without me
Chasing humanity's highest idols
Our names and our personalities
Will never lead you to enlightenment.
How much more simple can this be?

Song of Arirang

Leading us to the world of enlightenment;
Arirang, Arirang, Arariyo
Let us all ascend the hills of Arirang;
If you leave me and go away
Your feet will hurt before you've gone ten miles.

Arirang - Arirang is an ancient folk song of Korean tradition referring to the joy of finding one's true self.

Arirang Fantasy

I want to be the light
That breaks open the night
Tears down the curtain of despair
Illuninates the stage with the light of hope
Throws open the closed window
And breathes in the fresh air.

Sun rises to its glory
Casting away darkness
Dawn of a new age
Awaken everyone,
And rise.

For the beauty of the Earth
And priceless peace
Let us stand in force
And co-create the future
Fellow Earth-Humans, New Humans
Let us all realize
Love for Humanity, love for the Earth.

With Mago's Dream in our hearts
Let us recite the verses of ChunBuKyung
And sing the joyous song of Arirang
Let us ascend the hills of Arirang
Arirang, Arirang, Arariyo
Let us all ascend the hills of Arirang.

*ChunBuKyung - ChunBuKyung is an ancient Korean sacred
text, generally regarded to be more than 9,000 years old,
consisting of 81 letters summarizing the truth of heaven, earth,
and humanity.*

Earth Human

I have come to earth
With love in my heart
To deliver her
From sickness and disease;
For this I have come
With many upon many.

We feel the need
For a new spiritual culture
To blossom forth,
So that we may converse
With love for mother earth
In our hearts.

Through a Cultural Olympics
We shall raise our consciousness
For love of the earth
And love for humanity,
For an age in which all people
And religions will be accorded respect.

Holding the dream of a new birth
Of a beautiful earth,
A Spiritual United Nations
Will rise to heal the planet
That has suffered so
For our sake.

For love of the earth
We shall arise
Spiritually awakened

To truly become Earth-Humans;
Each person, a New Human
HongIkInGan.

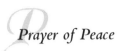

Prayer of Peace

I offer this prayer of peace
Not to any one god nor to many gods
Not to the Christian god
Nor to the Jewish god
Nor the Buddhist god
Nor the Islamic god
Not even to the indigenous gods of many nations
But to the divinity within us all
That makes us all brothers and sisters
To make us truly One Family
In the name of humanity.

I offer this prayer of peace
To the cosmic Oneness that is our birthright
Our privilege
And our strength
That should we let it shine and show us the way
Will guide us to the road of peace
Not the Christian peace
Not the Jewish peace
Not the Islamic peace
Nor the Buddhist peace
Not the indigenous peace of many nations
But the human peace
That has a place in the hearts of all people
To allow us to truly fulfill our divine potential
To become children of one humanity.

I offer this prayer of peace
To allow us all to realize
The truth of our existence

To discover
The sanctity of our lives
To seek
The spirituality of our beings
Please allow us to experience
With all our hearts and our souls
The intimate connection to the divine
Which we all posses inside
For our bodies are the temples of worship
And our souls the altars
Upon which we shall stand tall
And live out the true meaning
Of our existence.

I offer this prayer of peace
To declare a revolution
Of the human spirit
I wish to announce that
It is now time
For all of us to spiritually awaken
And become enlightened
That the time for an enlightened few is over
That the age of elitist enlightenment has passed
For how long will you seek for prophets
To come down from mountaintops
And tell us what to do.

We all must become enlightened
To recognize our divinity
To raise our consciousness
And proclaim our independence
From blind reliance on long ago sages
And draw the answers from our own well
Of spiritual wisdom

We must ourselves become the enlightened ones
We must ourselves realize our Oneness
I declare that we must all become 'Earth-Humans'
Of the earth
And not of any religion, nation or race
But of this earth, for this earth and by this earth
To create a lasting peace
On earth.

I offer this prayer of peace
For the United Nations
In which we stand today
To lift itself from the quicksand of politics
And live out its distinctly spiritual goal
To eradicate the disease of war
And create an equitable and peaceful world.
Let us hope that the UN finds
The strength and the will
To speak on behalf of all people of the earth
And not just for a few privileged nations
Let us wish upon the UN the wisdom
To become the beacon that we can all follow
To the promised land of love and peace
I pray to thee
God of all gods
Divine spirit that lives within us
And connects us in One Life
That you grant us the vision
To establish a Spiritual UN
That will guide us into the next millennium.

I offer this prayer of peace
With all my fellow 'Earth-Humans'
For a lasting peace on earth.

I offered this prayer at the Opening Ceremony of the Millennium World Peace Summit of Religious and Spiritual Leaders in the General Assembly Hall of the United Nations on August 28th, 2000.

Prayer for a Spiritual United Nations (SUN)

Night and day trade places
Sun and moon light up the stars
Yet the sun does not cast light.
The moon is not real
The stars are not true stars
For they fail to brighten our minds.

The world shines brightly
While our minds remain un-illuminated.
How long shall we live in darkness
When eternal truth lies herein?

No nation, creed, or religion is itself, the truth.

Truth lies within all.
Love the earth.
Love humanity.
Respect other cultures and spiritual traditions.

Such truths are the light
By which we can brighten our minds.
Such truths are the real sun, moon and stars.
Such truths are the beacon
From which our lives must be guided.
They comprise the beginning and the end
And have the power to save us.

Righteous people will rise up in all nations.
With divinity, wisdom and sympathy.
Separation of nation and religion
Will disappear into the setting sun

And new songs will rise
To signal the birth of a new earth village.

A village that will embrace
All nations, races and religions,
And will not remember
The killing and the bloodshed.
The time is ripe
For those who are ready will rise to the stage.

Blessings upon all who hear this message.

For the Spiritual Rebirth of America

America, your name speaks of greatness
Golden flower of the age, brightly shining
Great are your deeds and your achievements
Proud in your pioneering spirit
World's greatest might, wealth and pride;

Greater even than giants of the past
With freedom and promise of equality and peace
Welcoming people of all colors and creeds
To infinite opportunity
For infinite creation;

A dark shadow casts a pall upon this blessed land
Explosive tragedy aimed at your heart
Anger and fear
Sadness and despair
Felt by everyone, shared by all;

America, I beseech you
Use your strength, immeasurable and infinite
To turn this tragedy to opportunity
For your strength lies in justice and truth
In the hearts of all Americans;

Great soul of America
Awaken to the true meaning of your existence
And build a bridge upon which humanity may cross
Into a new age of eternal peace
Of a spiritual civilization;

Just as you have done in times past

You shall break through the darkness
Reborn as a golden flower in the garden of a new age
Of a spiritual civilization
To lead the world;

Leading nations and people alike
Born anew
Through tragedy turned to opportunity
For America is great unto herself
And complete.

This poem was written in the immediate aftermath of September 11, 2001 attack on NYC and D.C., and was read aloud to the audience at a lecture at MIT scheduled for the weekend of the fateful week.

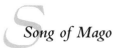

Song of Mago

Sons and daughters of Mago!
Rise from your sleep;
Like a lion roaring awake
A tiger bursting through the forest
Flowers blossoming on a withered branch
Let our passionate souls light the fire
For humanity!
For the Earth!

Upon the beauty of the Earth
Peace and joy fade away
Decay and decadence rule the day
Polluting the land;
Screams rise in the air
Moans of suffering and pain
Screams of anger and jealousy;
We must save
Our diseased Earth
Enfeebled humanity
Oh Earth-Human, New Human!

Beautiful earth and healthy humanity
We must have
Sons and Daughters of Mago awaken!
The future of Earth
The fate of humanity
Depends on what we now choose.
Why have we come to Earth?
Did you come to heal or to kill?

Beautiful earth and precious humanity

Whose sun yonder shines brightly?
The shimmering silver rays of the moon
And the stars blinking with wonderment
Ask this question
What will you give
For the beautiful Earth and humanity?

Let us all shout
Love for humanity!
Love for the Earth!
Let us now gather our strength
For the future of
Our Earth and humanity.

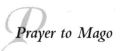

Prayer to Mago

Mago, Mother Earth
Our soul, our life, our ultimate source
For blessing us with your love
We thank you;

Mago, Mother Earth
For that blissful moment
Realizing that your soul is our soul
Rising together from the sea of love
Standing tall in a field of peace
We thank you;

Mago, Mother Earth
For your redeeming tears
Shed for needless suffering
Caused by foolish ideas of good and evil
Wrought by separation and judgment
We thank you;

Mago, Mother Earth
For your great love
Unconditional and unlimited
Despite our foolishness
Our fall from divine grace
We thank you;

Mago, Mother Earth
For your gift of enlightenment
Teaching us to heal
Helping us to grow
Allowing our recovery

We thank you;

Mago, Mother Earth
For our completion
Perfect in our divinity within
Joyful in harmony without
Secure in peace all around
We thank you.

Path to Heaven

Path to heaven
Where do you lie,
Path to heaven
Anywhere and everywhere
Open for all time
Closed only to the
Lazy and the fearful.

What we seek is beautiful and sublime,
What we seek is divine,
We seek
Spiritual growth.

Virtue
Exquisite beauty
Highest joy,
These can be attained
Through peace
Of heaven, earth and human.

If you seek to live
In the safety of the moment
Out of laziness and indolence
Fear and terror,
In the face of the dream for a new world
Thus is the path to heaven blocked.

The altar on which you speak to heaven
Shall manifest fully
Only when you have
Conquered laziness, idleness and fear,

Only when you strive
For virtue with all your heart,
Only when your beating heart
Merges with the rhythm of heaven,
Only when your soul and heaven's soul
Have become one.
I have experienced this
And seek to share.

This altar
Made of solitude
Solitude magnificent
With no place for shelter
Nothing to become aware of
With only your heart as your guide
You shall walk through heaven's gate.

Beyond those heavenly doors
Awaits the all-encompassing light
Of your existence,
A new world
Without time or place
Infinite.

I shall share my breath with many
To speak of a new world to come,
In a meeting of hearts and minds
In a gathering called *Meeting with Mago*.

When the full moon rises
Painting Sedona's red rocks crimson silver
Shining brightly under the stars
Let us meet with Mago,

Beyond religion and nationality
Let us gather
And speak of the soul.

Our meeting will begin history anew
Moving toward completion,
A culture of enlightenment
A civilization of the spirit,
Founding the SUN
With all hearts that seek
Spiritual completion
Soulful perfection
Together in sincerity.

A Shiny Emerald Tear

Wind blows
Foreboding and gloomy
Transporting blood and death
Within stormy bosom
Mouth stretched wide open
Swallowing the earth whole.

War brings
Death and suffering
With screams of victims
Light of hope fades
Hidden by the darkness of evil clouds.

Malignant stares of assassins
Haze of hatred in the air
Tears running in a river of revenge
Evil begets evil
Curses bear curses.

Why do these things continue?
Desire for peace
Immediate and bare
Mercy and love
Are these but lies?

Oh divine mercy
Promise of eternal peace
How long can the Earth continue
On this road of destruction
Leading to a black hole of obliteration?

Ah, this beauty of the cosmos
Sinking unseen into the Milky Way
This earth not of our own making
But victim of our destruction.

If only love for the Earth were to become
A giant teardrop of the color green
To drop onto the parched bosom of the Earth
Filled with rivulets of peace
Tears of peace and love
Precious drop of emerald green.

What sacred secret do you possess?
Sound of life echoing from that place deep within
Seat of the soul
This is where my hope shall live.

Sedona & Lake Powell, Wonder of the Cosmos

Last clean breath
Of the twenty-first century,
With heaviness in my heart
I gaze upon your splendor
As sickness envelops the earth.

Even the sun and moon
Are not permitted to linger
In the primitive beauty,
As I stand watching
This Indian holy ground
Colorado River passing beneath
The Rainbow Bridge.

Flowing ceaselessly through the desert
Revealing her past
Thousands turn to millions of years
Shimmering in the moonlight.
Heaven, earth and human become one
Whispering of an earth village.

History speaks of her incompletion
With warnings of doom
For the road we are on.
History speaks of her desire to be whole
Through lasting peace and harmony
Of a whole village
Of the earth.

From rainbow bridge
The divinity within us cries,

My daughters, my sons
Save this earth,
Awaken to the world
To all of humanity.

With the voice of divine suffering
Still in our hearts,
Let us now return to Sedona
And greet the rainbow
And the lake
And realize that we are all
Of this earth.

Songs of Sedona Mago Garden

As morning sun graces Sedona Mago Garden,
Red soil awakens to her calling
And birds noisily greet the dawn.

As zephyr stirs across the tree tops,
Leaves and grasses dance to the voices
Of Mother Earth whispering her love.

As evening sun sets on Sedona Mago Garden,
Secret Mountain yonder beckons with an embrace
Rejoicing in the golden, sacred light.

As stars twinkle above Sedona Mago Garden,
She merges into the eternal Nothingness
Drawing sacred beauty not of this world.

As moon glows upon Sedona Mago Garden,
Trees, lakes, and all life sing and dance in thanks
Inside the grandest spotlight of all.

Sedona Mago Garden houses three canyons
Chunhwa, Mago, and Senya;
Sedona Mago Garden hides three caves
Chunhwa, Mago, and Dangun;
Sedona Mago Garden embraces one lake
Dangun's Lake;
Sedona Mago Garden hosts twelve vortices.

Sedona Mago Garden veils that most sacred place of
     all
The Garden of Gods above Chunhwa Canyon,

A magical place where gods talk and plan of peace
Sending forth the divine energy
To awaken the souls in Sedona Mago Garden.

Sedona Mago Garden is the home
To people working to realize human health and peace
     healers.

As flowers cover the Earth with their beauty,
Let the power of the spiritual movement
Let the healing energy of the vortices
Radiate from Sedona Mago Garden
And cover the world.

SUN waits for us there
100 million strong healing community
Becoming one with Mother Earth
There lies our vision and dreams.

The first upon this Earth
A school to teach the Law of Heavenly Ascension
     (ChunHwa)
Path to divine healing on earth.

They are coming to Sedona Mago Garden
With dreams of healers
With dreams of peace
With Mago's Dreams
To love humanity and the Earth
They are coming to Sedona Mago Garden.

Our dreams
Mago's Dreams
Are One

And the same.

Mago's Dream will come true
Through Peace of the Power Brain.

Even today
A new day dawns
With joyous shouts and greetings
Of Mago's healers.

For You

I am here... with you.
I came to the earth
In search of you.
Without you I am blind
Not seeing who I am.
I am ignorant without you
Not knowing heaven and earth.
Without you I am confused,
Believing love and obsession
To be the same.

You have taught me life and peace
And given me dreams and hope.
You are my all, you are my love.
Wherever you beckon, I shall follow.
Whatever you ask of me, I shall do.
Whatever you desire, I shall become.

I hear your breath
In the sound of the wind.
I taste the sweetness of peace
In the bosom of the clouds.
My dream lies
In the completion of my soul.
My hope lives
For sharing love and peace.
You are my life
You are my all.
Wherever you live
I live.

You have taught me life and peace
And given me dreams and hope.
You are my all, you are my love.
Wherever you beckon, I shall follow.
Whatever you ask of me, I shall do.
Whatever you desire, I shall become.